How to be an African Lady

How to be an African Lady

Uche Onyebadi

Kenway Publications
Nairobi • Kampala • Dar es Salaam

Published by Kenway Publications
a subsidiary of
East African Educational Publishers Ltd
Brick Court, Mpaka Road/Woodvale Grove
Westlands, P.O. Box 45314
Nairobi

East African Educational Publishers Ltd.
Pioneer House, Jinja Road
P.O. Box 11542
Kampala

Ujuzi Educational Publishers Ltd.
P O. Box 31647, Kijito-Nyama
Dar es Salaam

© Uche Onyebadi: 1998
First published 1998

ISBN 9966-46-778-5

Printed in Kenya by Sunlitho Ltd.
P.O. Box 13939, Nairobi

Contents

Assessing other Ladies	1
How to Go Back to a Boyfriend (after a quarrel)	4
Office Ethics	7
How to Walk	10
Handbag Ritual	13
Being the Boss	15
How to be Startled	18
What to do When Broke	21
Boyfriends	23
Sex	25
Being a Mistress	26
Meeting the other Woman (in your man's house)	28
Being a Senior Girl	30
Beauty Tips	32
Agelessness	36
Attitude Towards Marriage	38
Expected Courtesies	40
Taxi Lessons (in countries where two or more people can share a taxi)	44
Accepting A Ride	46
What to Read; What to Watch	49
Out for Lunch	51
Going Shopping	54
Being Chased	57
When to Hiss	59
Going For A Weekend	61
Talking Big	63
How to Speak	66
Home and Alone	69
What should make a Lady Happy	72
A Lady's Prayer	74

Assessing Other Ladies

African ladies are the best assessors of their folk. Men look at women and only see glamour; women look at themselves with the power of an x-ray equipment and see what the male eyes don't often figure out.

Assessing other ladies is one of the favourite pastimes of the modern African lady. This assessment is not exactly called gossip, although the difference is hard to spot, by men!

There are no fixed rules about assessing ladies. But a common trend among the various forms of assessment is that the assessors should first take a comprehensive look at the lady being assessed before they commence business.

Take the example of this bus stop scenario. Two ladies are waiting for a bus. Another lady comes along and walks past them. Both ladies follow her with their eyes until the other lady is completely out of sight.

Then they turn and look at each other conspiratorially, smile coyishly and immediately launch their missiles.

"Did you see that *girl*? You would think she owns the world. The late Diana, Princess of Wales couldn't have done better. People just make me laugh," says the first lady.

"Don't mind that *notice me* girl. Did you see the 13th century shoes she wore?" puts in the other one.

"I didn't know you saw them too. How can a modern lady put on such great-grandma's shoes?"

"And her calves, did you see them?"

"Ouch! I thought she was carrying a ten-pound tuber of yam instead of a calf. The thing is quite embarrassing."

"Did you take a good look at her hair?"

"Of course. I wonder when she last saw a hairdresser."

"I wonder too. Come, did you notice she wore this cheap, foul-smelling perfume?"

"My sister, who wouldn't notice such foul smell."

"I could bet a million she was covering some foul smell."

"Of course. You must know Nike. She wears a similar perfume because of her deadly odour."

"Nike, body odour? No wonder she is always in and out of the *ladies*. And to think that it's the same Nike who carries herself as if she is the first lady at the White House in Washington DC."

"Don't bother about that one. She's just like her friend, Mercy, who probably has the illusion that she's the most brilliant person around, just because she got a *first class degree in computer science*."

"First class degree my foot! With all her first class rubbish she can't even dress properly."

"Dressing? That one's a non-starter. Her colour combination is worse than horrible. Do you know she wore a purple blouse and a green skirt to the office yesterday?"

"I'm not surprised. But, she is no better than her colleague, Gladys."

"Ah! That one makes me sick. She shouldn't be called a lady at all. Isn't she the girl whose boobs are so frighteningly *extra large* that they can easily be tucked away right down into her skirt?"

"That's her. And she feels she is the best thing that happened to womanhood just because she was born in London and carries a British passport."

"Don't take her seriously. She's just like Tessy who was born in New York but can't speak simple, correct English. She thinks speaking *slang* is the *real thing*."

"Tessy, born in New York? I can't believe it. She is so local that you would think she's lived in the village all her life."

"And Florence too. She was born in Canada but all she knows is to hop into bed with practically all the directors in her office."

"No wonder she continues to be promoted rapidly. Anyway, Angela does the same thing."

"*That one* is no better than a registered prostitute. I even wonder what men see in her. Is it her elephant-size behind or her flabby breasts or the fact that she is as short as the pigmies of the Congo forest?"

"She's a cheap girl, just like Benedicta who is a specialist in husband-snatching."

"But Benedicta can't be worse than Susan who snatched her own sister's husband!"

"They are all the same. Ah! Look at that girl coming this way. She walks like a hungry hyena."

"That's true. But she might as well be a lunatic for all you care. Life has become so tough these days that you really cannot be sure of anyone's sanity."

"I agree with you, my sister. In fact, we should get out of here. Can you see those ladies to your left? They've been staring at us as if they are jealous of our dresses."

"There comes the bus, let's dash in. These women could be deadly."

Assessing other ladies thrills many a modern lady. What she should know but cares very little about is that others are assessing her too. Indeed, one of her assessors could just be the lady who had teamed up with her to assess others!

How To Go Back To A Boyfriend
(after a quarrel)

African boyfriends are supposed to be lousy lovers. They don't know *how to treat a lady*! They feel they have a natural right to be worshipped by women. For this reason, they deserve to be put in their proper position, especially in a post-Beijing era! And what better way is there for a nice lady to check men's arrogance than to call their bluff and wait for the inevitable quarrels that shall follow!

A decent and realistic lady must be prepared to quarrel with her boyfriend, if only to teach him a lesson or two in African *ladyhood*.

The only risk in administering these lessons is that some of these boyfriends, if only to maintain their pride and masculine *superiority complex*, may not want to initiate a reconciliation. And the estrangement could end up becoming permanent.

But, African ladies are usually capable of any task, so getting a recalcitrant boyfriend back should pose no problem.

At the dawn of one of those quarrels, an imaginative lady should be able to *guard her pride jealously*. She must not send the man any *I'm sorry* cards, unless he makes the first move. Should he even come around and try to make amends, the courageous lady should unreservedly *tell him off*, especially if her friends happen to be around. *I'm fed up with you and I think I'm through with this relationship*, is a standard way of telling him off. But the lady must be careful not to sound emphatic or say those words with an air of finality. They must be said in such a way as to convey the message that the man can only rekindle the relationship by persevering in his plea for a reconciliation.

If the man is the stubborn type and shows no sign of remorse or trying to stage a come-back, the wise lady need not worry (if she is still keen on maintaining the relationship) for *there are several ways to kill this rat called the African man!*

The lady may first send one or two of her female friends - those known to her man - to *strongly protest* the way he has been maltreating *our friend*. Actually, their real mission should be to make a subtle plea for him to go and *beg* her. Afterall, they chip in, *you know how we women behave!*

Should this strategy not work, the lady should go directly to the man's male friends and engineer them to intercede or *talk some sense into him*, without making it appear as if she sent them.

The next step - if things are still not okay - is to visit the man's house when the lady is beyond all *reasonable and unreasonable doubts* certain that he is not at home. She should *play* with his younger brothers and sisters, generally *look around* and leave just when she is sure he is about to return. She must resist all temptations to drop him a note - but must make sure that everybody in the house will tell *my brother* the story about how auntie came, *played and stayed long* with us, and left *not quite long before you returned.*

If the man is still buried in his stubbornness, the lady can *drop by* in his office when he is due for lunch break. But she must not agree to be taken out for lunch (although she may wish for exactly that). She can hide under the disguise that she just happened to be *passing by* when, for *God's sake,* she decided *to pop in and say hi,* just to find out if he was *still alive.* She must disappear thereafter. No amount of persuasion should make her stay and listen to his possible apologies. At best, she should inform him that *if you want me, you know where to find me.*

The final strategy - if all plans fail - is to visit his house when the lady is sure he is indoors. She should enter the house, give him no more than a condescending nod - ignoring him is preferable - but go ahead and greet every other person around most heartily. Then, she should walk across to the flowerpots, examine the flowers and water them if necessary, mumbling something about how they have withered just in her *brief absence.*

Unless the man's heart is made of cast-iron, he might at this point try to be friendly by moving closer to her. A perceptive lady should know at this point that she has won the game. But, she should prop up her pride by gesturing and warning him to *please don't touch me.* That should be the time to declare that she didn't come to see him; that the purpose of her visit was to make sure the flowers did not die, if not, you *wouldn't find me here!*

Normally, the man calls for a truce at this point and the lady, still wearing an apparently stern countenance, would smile inwardly as if to say: *trust me to twist him around my little finger!*

Office Ethics

African men have a way of doing things. So do their ladies. In the office, a genuine lady must not allow herself to be unnecessarily inhibited by the official rules of conduct. Most of the time, it is the men who draw up these regulations. That being the case, most of these office rules hardly take cognisance of the special needs of ladies. It is therefore reasonable and logical for ladies to have extra codes that should guide their behaviour in their offices.

Take reporting for duty on time for instance. This is something no lady should aspire to accomplish. The reason is simple. A lady needs plenty of time to dress up in the morning. There is the one-hour period that is spent in the bathroom. Then another one hour

for applying her make-up. There is another forty-five minute period of self-admiration in front of her mirror. Choosing the right clothes, handbag and shoes, consumes a great deal of time too. How on earth is a lady expected to accomplish all that between 6.30 a.m. when she wakes up and 7.30 a.m. or 8.00 a.m. when she ought to report for work, *according to men's regulations?*

Unlike ladies, men wake up, rush through everything including breakfast and dash off to work. This does not require much time. Since ladies therefore have more personal items on their early morning agenda, it is perfect to arrive late in the office!

Once in the office, a mature lady's desk needs not be unnecessarily littered with files and other implements she is supposed to work with. All of them can be tucked away in the drawers where they belong. A decent lady's table should contain the following items (among others): a small mirror she'll look at from time to time to make sure that her face glitters at all times; her photographs taken preferably in Europe or the USA; an ashtray if she smokes; one or two tiny flower-pots; and some fashion and gossip magazines.

A lady ought to go to work with a handful of novels. Most of the time, office work is quite a boring exercise. The thing to do therefore is to read the novels, most of which should have romantic themes. In between reading a few chapters, the lady may also consider it fit to do some real boring work - like looking at her in-tray!

It should be a standard practice for a lady to visit the *ladies* as frequently as possible during office hours. What she does there should be of no concern to men. Suffice it to say, however, that each time she emerges from one of her toilet sessions, her face should noticeably be retouched with powder, lipstick, mascara et cetera.

It should also be a standard office practice to stay for hours on end on the telephone. Official calls should not last more than a few minutes. Personal calls are the juicy part of phone calls and no less than thirty minutes should be spent on each of them. Of course, anyone who complains should be told straightaway to mind his own business!

If the lady is a secretary, it should be her eternal duty to ensure that no one reaches her boss either on phone or physically. Every visitor must first tell the lady his or her business with the boss. If the lady is not impressed, the visitor should be told to go away. *Hoarding* the boss is a primary function of lady secretaries. A measure of how hard she has worked lies on the number of people she has prevented from having access to her boss!

Lunch time is sacred. Every lady must observe it in her office. No matter how urgent something needs to be done in the office, a lady should never sacrifice her lunch time for it. Even if she is not going out for lunch, the lady should occupy her time reading novels, sleeping or chatting. The job can always wait.

Of course a lady must leave the office right on time, if not earlier. Thirty minutes before closing time, she should disappear into the toilet once more and get ready for home. Shame on the lady who leaves her office looking as ruffled as a Bosnian refugee!

How To Walk

Real African ladies don't just walk; they swagger. Those who make it a habit to walk are no ladies. They are uncultured and unsophisticated. And they inflict inestimable injury on *ladyhood*. To be a lady is to master the art of walking properly; to take those elegant and provocative strides that compel all male eyes to have a second look at the lady passing by. Indeed, if a lady walks past and the men around do not follow her with their eyes - the way dogs gape at and follow the movement of meat or bone - then the lady is no lady at all. She just can't walk properly!

In order to walk the way a well-groomed lady should, a lady has to acquire a pair of very high-heeled shoes. The higher and more needle-like the heels, the more they facilitate compelling strides . Secondly, the wearing of very tight-fitting dresses, especially those that have an iron-grip on the knees, enables the lady to walk majestically.

These items - the high-heeled shoes and tight-fitting dresses - are gems for enabling faultless strides because they, in the first place, make it impossible for their wearers to walk naturally. So, the more unnatural the strides, the more the lady's adroitness on how a modern lady ought to walk.

Now, to the main thing. Steps should be taken in halves. These half-steps further impede movement and accentuate the ability to walk perfectly! Only an awkward walker takes the full strides she is endowed with.

When these short strides are being made, the lady should throw out her legs at 75 degrees (not 90 degrees, for it would amount to walking naturally). So, the left leg goes 75 degrees and the right does the same. The whole idea is to be seen walking in an X - formation.

Walking and the jolly swinging of the backside are inseparable. It thus means that to walk *correctly*, a lady even if she is as skinny as a hunger-ravaged refugee- with little or barely pronounced behind-should swing it as if she is carrying a mountain there. The x-formation walking pattern only serves to catalyse the pendulum-like swings that the backside must make.

All ladies who intend to excel in *how to walk* should endeavour to be present at beauty pageants or fashion exhibitions. Those models who take part in fashion and beauty shows are in most cases well mastered on how to walk on stage. They even swing their shoulders, for in the process, their backsides are made more elastic in their swings too. This is what is called the *cat-walk*; something directly learnt from cats!

The true African lady should always walk *properly* in public . This presupposes that she must not run! Even when the clouds are gathering, a *complete* lady must swagger on. That is the core of the philosophy of walking.

A lady, therefore, must not run across the road, no matter how busy it is. She must wait - even if it takes hours - until she cannot see any approaching vehicle before she swaggers across the road. If she is in a hurry, she can board a taxi and make a three-kilometre U-turn in order to be dropped exactly opposite where she was standing. This is what is called *decorum*. But all rules, especially in an African country, have their exceptions. Sometimes, it might be permissible for a lady to run a little bit while crossing the road. In this case however, she has to demonstrate the beauty of how ladies should run in public. She may grab her breasts as if to prevent them from falling off, or clutch her hand-bag feverishly, and saunter across the road in the name of running! The only time a lady should run like an Olympic gold medalist is when she sees a snake or when one of those Lagos *molue* buses that have no brakes, or those *matatus* of Nairobi city whose drivers are under the firm influence of the local brew called *changaa,* suddenly appear while she is undertaking the ritual of crossing the road.

Post script: *A lady must not walk a long distance. She might get tired of swinging her backside or forget it momentarily while men are still watching. If, however, there is a long distance to cover, she must carry a pair of slippers in her polythene bag so that when she is out of public glare, she can put them on and walk without embellishing her strides. Such slippers are also handy in offices where she might have to walk around without people paying her any attention.*

Handbag Ritual

Without a handbag, a modern lady may not exactly know what to do with her arms. Both items - arms and the handbag - have become so inseparable that to carry a handbag has become something of a ritual as well as an obsession to the ladies of contemporary Africa. A lady, therefore, carries a handbag - although she may not need anything inside it - for as long as whatever gathering she is attending lasts.

Hand-bag carrying, nonetheless, pre-dates the modern lady. Women have always carried them. But, the difference between women and ladies lies in the reason for carrying them.

The pre-modern women saw it primarily as temporary warehouses where things like biscuits, groundnuts, pieces of bread and similar sundry items, distributed at family or club meetings were stored for the kids at home. So, as soon as mother returned from an outing, the kids made straight for her hand-bag in anticipation of these delicacies. The secondary use for the handbags then was to keep mundane items like *scent* (now called perfume), handkerchiefs that were rarely used, and chaplets and Bibles for church. Nothing more.

For the modern lady, the handbag is an essential part of her dressing. A hand-bag is therefore something hung around the arms *to match* the dress. So, in choosing a handbag, a lady has to be careful to select the one that would match her dress. A modern lady's handbag is not the type of warehouse it used to be years ago. Today, it serves other purposes.

Something noteworthy about a lady's handbag is the fact that a man must not be allowed to look inside and see its contents. The fact that ladies relish *searching* men's briefcases is irrelevant. Naturally, any man caught probing a lady's handbag deserves all the insults he would get for the deed.

If you are looking for a lady's *Swiss bank*, try her handbag. But, nobody shall be privileged to know how much money she has there.

So, while she might be crying over lack of money and begging you for some, her *Swiss bank* might indeed be over-spilling with money!

A few items that find their way into a lady's hand-bag may include:

- a. An address book which contains the most secret and intimate names which mean a lot.
- b. Secret love notes that must not be seen by another pair of eyes.
- c. An emergency beauty-kit.
- d. Some junk, including pens that have long been out of use.
- e. A number of personal items, including, possibly, an inner wear, just in case an unscheduled *night-shift* at a boyfriend's becomes imperative.
- f. Other things which are of no use to men.

Being The Boss

For too long, cultural inhibitions have held African ladies in captivity. But to a large extent, education has helped liberate these ladies. However, the process of liberation or emancipation, as ladies fancifully call their *struggle*, still goes on. In this regard, a modern lady should always dream about being the boss someday, with men, many of them, under her command.

An intelligent lady ought to grasp the full impact of - and know exactly- how to be a boss, both at home and the office.

Being the boss at home - in the matrimonial home - is usually a tough achievement. Men, the reputably arrogant and selfish African men, never want to give up or even delegate part of their leadership role in the home. But modern-day economics is threatening men's claims to the home presidency. Where the lady is the bread-winner (and the man is probably unemployed), the working lady has a perfect set-up for a *coup d'etat*. She must not waste any time assuming the command of the home. There is no point being diplomatic about being in charge. She must move in and claim the home leadership at the speed with which Nigerian army officers execute a *coup d'etat*

Being the boss at home entails making the man pay for all his years of foolery and arrogance. A nice lady should know how much *pocket money* she doles out to her retrenched or economically battered man. It must not be too much, lest he begins to use the money to finance his amorous escapades. Any day he gets swollen-headed and makes the lady mad, literally, his allowance must be stopped automatically. It also pays great dividends for the lady to constantly remind him that she is in charge. He can only be properly put in his place with such reminders. Beating about the bush can never sober him up.

Of course, the man has to be made to be realistic and properly adjust to the new dispensation. Household chores may have been a taboo to him in the past; now, they shall be part of his daily routine.

However, being the boss in the office is a different thing altogether. Here, the relationship is impersonal and should strictly be treated as such. Right from the outset, everybody in that office has to be unequivocally clear that the lady is a no-nonsense person. If the lady discovers that people call her an iron-lady in remembrance of Britain's erstwhile Prime Minister Margaret Thatcher, all the better for her image. A lady-boss has to be seen to be tough and uncompromising. She has to instill a sense of fear in all subordinate workers. If this entails shouting at them, a lady just has to shout. If it means issuing queries and suspending people from work at the flimsiest excuse, let the queries and letters of suspension flow!

Lady-bosses are always vulnerable to being taken for granted, so a lady must avoid this by being resolute in her actions. No amount of cajoling or appeal should make her change her decision. A person who has been issued a query has to write a reply. A person suspended from duty has just to serve his or her punishment. Should the person show any inclination toward stubbornness, a dismissal should follow.

To have a successful reign as a boss, a lady has to be decisive on how she relates to men and women who work with her in the following manner.

Men: Her philosophy should be that all men have to be cut down to size. Better to have a man as the office attendant so that he can be sent on as many errands as possible - to buy things like Coca-Cola and chewing gum for the boss. All work done by men has to be thoroughly scrutinised and any error noticed must be pointed out in such a way as to make men look stupid. While addressing them, her tone should be harsh and condescending. Their opinions do not deserve attention and they should be overworked. That is the only way they would recognise who the boss is!

Women: Women may be more difficult to deal with. The first lesson, however, is that the lady-boss should be strict when dealing with them. Find some fault in all they do. The prettier the woman is, the more the need to be ruthless with her. Any day such a woman wears a remarkably beautiful dress to the office, or sports a striking hair-do, or puts on attractive and expensive shoes, bangles etc., that should be the day she shall be more thoroughly tongue-lashed and her attitude to work condemned. The number of male visitors she receives should be cut down. Better still, such visits should be stopped altogether. She should be instructed to restrict the visits to her home. All women who work with the lady-boss should be prepared to be humiliated from time to time in order to have a smooth working relationship with her.

How To Be Startled

Being startled is serious business. Any lady who cannot be properly startled diminishes her feminity. She could as well do away with that softness ladies are associated with. People might even begin to wonder whether she is actually a lady or a mere *woman*; a woman being one of those females from the hintherland who are yet to have access to what modern civilisation has abundantly bestowed on her counterparts in the city.

A true African lady, especially if she resides in the big metropolis, must always be open to stimuli that shaould startle her. Nearly everything shall come as a surprise. But her counterparts in the rural areas need not be susceptible to being startled for men would

be too busy in their farms anyway to notice the metamorphosis in them. For a lady, being startled loses its planned effect when no one appreciates the drama that accompanies it.

A glimpse of the contingency list of such *startlers* should amplify this point. A lady shall be *genuinely* startled (in public) when:

a. She notices a harmless insect on her dress.
b. A spider suddenly crosses her path or is sighted afar.
c. She comes across a gory scene while reading a novel.
d. A cockroach suddenly jumps out of her drawer in the office.
e. There is an unanticipated outburst of wind at an open-air party.
f. She unexpectedly finds her misplaced make-up kit.
g. Someone slaps her at the back in a crowded party.
h. She discovers it is past closing time from work.
i. Her handkerchief slips off her grip at a cocktail.
j. A man offers to take her out for lunch.

A necessary aspect of being startled is having the ability to demonstrate that ephemeral shock one has gone through. This is a fundamental point which must not be ignored for being startled is a public affair which ought to attract some attention.

Should a spider come into the room where the lady is sitting, a torrent of *"what's that!", what's that!"* said in a surprised tone should be an appropriate reaction. An *ouch* would do when a piece of paper drops on her feet. When a lady suddenly notices a lunatic nearby, she should feverishly clutch her chest and scream an *oh my Gad!* An *oops* should be adequate when the wrong file is pulled out of the cabinet.

A lady should be able to tell the story of how she was startled, *startled* all the way as she tells it. And the story must be told in such graphic details that listeners should see the incident as quite extraordinary although in truth, it may be quite commonplace. So, the story about how a bee stormed into an office, buzzed around for a while before making its exit - all within fifteen seconds - should take not less than five minutes to tell. If her listeners are manifestly bored, the lady should ignore their expressions and continue to tell her wonderful tale!

Being startled is a great public show which must not be carried out at home, unless there are visitors there who need to be taught the beauty and wisdom of this act. When at home and alone - or with relatives - a lady should not waste her time and energy dramatising being startled. Should one of those big rats which are easily confused for rabbits or cats try to dash across the room, the same lady who was frightened to death on seeing a spider in her office, will pursue the rat and kill it, all alone!

What To Do When Broke

Being broke is an experience women generally go through. Or, so they try to make men believe. But the ability to disentangle oneself from the stranglehold of penury makes the difference between a *mere woman* and a lady. Women, when broke, wait for the heavens to rain down manna. They could wait forever. But ladies show no patience for such waiting, neither do they believe that manna still rains in this age. So, they take care of that penury.

Some so-called ladies trade their *ladyhood* for cash when they are broke. These are the ladies who still cling onto the old-fashioned ways of doing things. The truth is that a modern African lady does not really need to defile herself just because she wants some cash. There are different ways of skinning a cat and ladies are experts at solving financial problems without necessarily going through humiliating encounters.

The most fundamental thing any reasonable and rational lady should do when broke is to reach for her diary and search for those telephone numbers she wouldn't ordinarily call. If the call goes through, that would be her luck! The call would take such a tune:

"May I speak with Bayo, please?" she says in a sonorous voice.

"This is Bayo, who's speaking?"

"Jennifer. *Baayyyooo*! So you've completely forgotten me? Who's *dat gal* who has been spinning off your head?"

"No, come off it. You know how busy I am."

"Sorry, I've forgotten you are married to your job. Anyway, I've been dying for a drink all this time you've made yourself scarce."

"Jennifer baby! O.K. Let's make it tomorrow evening."

"Aren't you a darling!"

Two or three similar calls to other *Bayos* would be enough to pull her out of her penury. If the Bayos don't *play ball*, there are Uncles Timi and Jaiye-Jaiye whom she hasn't spoken to in several months. Just a call to these would do a lot of magic. They'll protest being neglected by their *stubborn niece* but will end up contributing to the lady's economic recovery fund.

Aunties are more difficult to convince to part with their money. Afterall, they too had played ladies in their prime! They should only be called in extreme situations.

When a lady is broke but wants to have a *decent* lunch, the idea is to hang around somewhere, ostensibly waiting for someone or something. Chances are that a fun-seeking man would pick her up *for a drink*. It is then up to her to extract lunch from the fun-seeker. Thereafter, she should pick up his address, give a a false name and address, promise to call him before the sun sets or rises, and then disappear! It is that simple!!

Whenever a lady is broke, it pays for her to dress elegantly. By doing this, she will be able to corner a few *catches* who will be just too glad to part with their money for as much as a peck from her! Besides, when she is immaculately dressed, she will be able to attract some loans whose repayment she can twist around her little finger. To be penniless and appear like a chief mourner is double tragedy. Those who do this are no ladies - they are *mere women*.

When a lady is broke, she must be selective in the type of discussions she gets involved in . She should feign a serious headache if there are hints that someone is planning a picnic and she is likely to be called upon to contribute and be part of it. Alternatively, she could lie that her boyfriend will be taking her out at the time of the picnic.

A boyfriend could become the saviour when a lady is broke. But, this should be done with some finesse. As soon as he steps into her house, the lady should welcome him with a flurry of *darling, sweetie pie and honey*. During their conversation, she should distract attention with a *guess what I saw today*. Of course he wouldn't guess right. He is then told of this elegant dress she saw in a boutique and was *dying* to own. Mr. Boyfriend will get the message!

Boyfriends

Outwardly, a good lady should insist that boyfriends are a nuisance; that she could do without them. But inwardly, she definitely thinks differently. All her efforts to look sophisticated and pretty are aimed, amongst other things, at catching the male attention and fishing out a boyfriend from their midst.

Having a boyfriend, however, is no spectacular achievement. Any woman can do that. What distinguishes a lady from a woman is that while the latter believes in holding tenaciously to a boyfriend, a lady must be able to have a fast turn-over of boyfriends. While the woman is prepared to tolerate *a whole load of rubbish* from her boyfriend, a lady must not have any patience for such arrant nonsense. Being independent-minded, she should be able to stand up to any boyfriend and *tell him off* when and where appropriate. If such an attitude leads to the severance of their relationship, the lady should not be perturbed as she would have a list of other potential boyfriends ready and waiting to be given an opportunity to call her *darling!*

To a lady, having a boyfriend should be more like a status symbol. The emotional aspect of it should be pushed aside. That, precisely, is why a lady should be highly selective when it comes to having boyfriends. Those who have not *made it* in life in one way or another should not stand any chance to be her boyfriend.

Since her boyfriends should be people of substance, it pays a lady to brag about them. In official and private discussions, she should slip in one or two things said or done by her boyfriend. If her dress, for instance, is commended, it should be a veritable chance to tell everyone that her dress was bought by her boyfriend during one of his numerous world tours! Should such comments irk her listeners, the lady should not *give a damn*. Oftentimes, those who wish she stopped talking about her boyfriend are just jealous!

It is necessary that a lady should have a variety of boyfriends who should serve various purposes. A military or police boyfriend is necessary so that the lady can feel confident to threaten to *deal with* her foes and casual adversaries. A businessman boyfriend plays the provider of all the money she would need to maintain her expensive taste. An actor or popular figure boyfriend is also necessary so that she can be seen at the *correct* circles in town. A lady is free to have as many boyfriends as she desires.

The very juicy aspect of the boyfriend business is a lady's ability to snatch her girlfriends' boyfriends. Until a lady successfully does this, it would be foolhardy for her to consider herself as being in the *big league* of ladies.

Next to *boyfriend-snatching*, a lady who has not made her numerous boyfriends clash in her house has not made her mark. Only immature ladies think the world would collapse when their boyfriends fortuitously meet each other in her house.

The overriding consideration in having a boyfriend must lie in his *utilitarian* value. Any boyfriend who has *nothing to offer* in tangible terms should be shown the door!

Sex

A lady who really understands and appreciates what it means to be a decent lady must not make sex an issue for public discussion.

She has to twitch each time the word is mentioned. Better still, she ought to move out of any circle where it is being discussed. She should only unchain her emotions about sex when and where privacy offers itself.

Being A Mistress

To the modern African lady, being a mistress is *no big deal*. Several years ago, it used to be considered a piece of immorality and mistresses were looked upon as no better than whores. They were called a variety of pejorative names, from husband-snatchers to family wreckers. In fact, what the modern lady has successfully done is to cleanse *mistresshood* of its rotten image and show it as an institution of honour and prestige.

As far as the lady is concerned, *mistress* is a word that should not even apply to her. It is a word that should be expunged from the dictionary. Her conviction is that she has a man who professes to love her. Now, if that same man happens to be married to another woman, too bad! And the rationale is simple; if the man was getting all the love and attention a wife should and can give a man, there wouldn't have been any need for him to look outside his home in the first place. So, the mistress is actually filling a big vacuum in the man's life!

The best thing about being a mistress, in the consideration of any intelligent lady, is that she knows where she stands with the man. He is not like other unmarried men who will swear to marry her, only to leave her house and make similar pledges to other ladies.

As a mistress, the lady is aware that marriage is virtually ruled out of the relationship, unless her aspiration is to be wife number two - which many ladies wouldn't want to be. So, her ambition is to have a good relationship and enjoy it while it lasts.

To accept to be a mistress, a sensible lady must insist on certain conditionalities. She has to be *mobile*. One flashy car would do, as it would be awkward for a lady to be seen walking about in the hot African sun. If the man is interested in the lady being immaculately dressed, he has to buy her a car. Or, at least be her chauffeur. That is one of the costs of keeping a mistress.

Another conditionality which the mistress should insist upon is for the man to get her a tastefully furnished apartment in a nice area of the city. Again, the logic is simple: If, because her *love* is unfortunately married to another woman and she, as a result, cannot visit him at home, then it's only reasonable that he has to provide her with adequate accommodation. Alternatively, if she already has her own apartment, then *Mr Loverman* should take over the payment of the rent.

To make a success of *mistresshood*, a lady needs to be tough and resolute in her dealings with her man. The reason is that there is another force at home competing for his love and loyalty. He should therefore be made to owe allegiance to the mistres first, and to his family afterwards. In fact, the wiser thing for the mistress to do is to take total control of the man's emotions and senses so that the family can only get the crumbs that fall from her table.

African *madams* have a way of sniffing out where their husbands' mistresses reside. Against all advice, they always go to the mistress's havens and try to warn them to keep off their husbands. Should the madam visit, a good mistress should give the woman a piece of her mind. Madam should be told to go and learn how to keep a man happy. The lady should claim that but for her effort, her *darling* would have suffered some emotional imbalance. She could also drop hints that her man has even promised her everything, including marriage. Then, madam should be thoroughly abused.

Thereafter, a reasonable lady should get in touch with her lover and complain amidst sobs that *your wife came here to insult me. You better come quickly and explain things to me. I can't stand being insulted by a frustrated woman just because I love you.* When the man appears, she may shed some tears to show how hurting the insults were.

Of course the man has to be made to apologise - by quarreling with his wife and handing in a full report to his mistress. Then, he has to give his lady a decent treat.

Meeting The *Other* Woman
(in your man's house)

An old-fashioned lady usually runs wild when she steps into her man's house and sees another lady with him. There might be a fight if tempers are not held in check. Whatever the scenario might be, that house cannot *contain* the three of them. Invariably, the old-fashioned lady raises as much dust as she can, to drive away the intruder.

A modern lady should not have time for such hassles. Meeting the other lady in her man's house is something that should not give her any nightmares. Unlike the old-fashioned lady, the modern ones have a firm way of handling the situation.

When a lady walks into the house and sees her rival, the first reaction should be to take a hard and long condescending look at the intruder, hiss and walk past her into the room. The intruder does not merit being talked to!

Thereafter, the lady shall show her familiarity with the house to the new lady. She should call her man inside the room and warn him to *get rid of that thing before I lose my cool*. Then, she should emerge and establish her ownership of the man and the house. She should zoom into the kitchen for coffee, adjust the television aerial or change the channels, switch on the video, go to the refrigerator for ice cream or a drink, telephone a friend for a long, relaxed chat and saunter in and out of the sitting room at will. Then she should loudly announce to her boyfriend that she is going to have her bath and inquire if he has had anything to eat.

Like a perambulator, the lady should come out again to ask her boyfriend if he saw her night-gown, claiming that *I can't find it where I left it just before we left for work this morning*. Then, she disappears into the room once more.

It is also when the other lady is around that a lady with some class should reactivate all the endearments she no longer uses in reference to her boyfriend. Things like *darling, how was work today* and *honey, what would you like to have for dinner*, should be lavishly poured out in front of the new lady.

It is also in front of the other lady that *honey* should be reminded that the Petersons had invited them over for lunch or that they were due to go to a particular club that weekend. To add spice to the tales, stories about what happened where they had an outing the previous weekend could be told in a flash.

The modern lady should consider it belittling to charge at the other lady because she did not invite herself to the house. When the intruder leaves, the man should face the confrontation of his life.

When a lady meets her rival, it is important for her to keep her charm and dignity by ignoring the gatecrasher. It is perhaps when the same *gal* makes another call that she should be taken aside and told in very clear language that she is on a suicide mission!

Being A Senior Girl

A lady graduates into the senior girl's cadre with the passage of years. This is the time when age puts her at a disadvantage and she does everything possible to conceal how old she is. It is a period when her make-up kit is her best companion. It is also a time for stock-taking.

To qualify as a senior girl, a lady has to live in a measure of comfort. She must have a good job with an attractive salary package. Her apartment has to look gorgeous. There has to be a car to the bargain; preferably one of those flashy ones that interminably roll out of Japan's car factory lines.

The route to becoming a senior girl is relatively easy to ply. In her younger days, a lady must not yield to any pressure which would get her permanently attached to any man, especially one who drops hints about possible marriage. While in school, she has to distance herself from her male classmates for they do not befit her romantic status. She would rather date well established men, possibly those who are already married and would not bother her with suggestions about a conjugal union. After successfully discouraging her peers, a lady should go ahead and enjoy her life to the fullest until it dawns on her that the time for *senior-girlhood* has come.

A senior girl might be a single parent. But, she should not take this as a stringent condition. Rather, vivaciousness is something she has to cling on to. She has to learn and master ways to enjoy herself. Although she has to have a chain of men in her life, men who are older in age, a respectable senior girl should endeavour to get herself a younger and nice looking man she should be seen around with. This serves dual purposes; to convince the world that she can still catch prize fishes when she switches on her charm and it gives her a soothing feeling of being younger as she enjoys re-living the best moments of her younger life.

A wise senior girl ought to treat her young man as delicately as she would handle an egg. If the young man cannot afford the basic necessities of life, they should be made available to him. He has to be dazzled with assorted gifts and showered with affection. On the overall, he has to be made to feel that he is in command of the relationship, if only to massage his ego.

Should some of the senior girl's friends disapprove of her relationship with her *prince charming*, she should just ignore their protestations. Most of them complain out of jealousy and inability to catch such young, ripe apples.

It is in this period of being a senior girl that a lady must endeavour to remember her maker, God. This is to pay back for the time she was younger and swept off her feet by the sizzling side of life and little or no time would have been devoted to God and his heavenly kingdom. Having remembered God at this dusk of her life, a lady should start attending churches or mosques with renewed fervour. Who knows, she could just find her Mr Right in those places!

One must confess that being a senior girl is a relatively new phenomenon in Africa. However, it is rapidly winning *converts*. That is why a lady must aspire to belong to this *new age*.

Beauty Tips

The primary lesson African ladies have learnt about beauty in modern times is that it is no longer in the *eyes of the beholder*. A lady must strive to look beautiful in the eyes of everybody! Anything short of this is being ugly.

Generally, ladies have two types of beauty; achieved and ascribed. Achieved beauty is man-made. This is what nearly all ladies possess in contemporary times. Ascribed beauty is a natural endowment. Few ladies have it these days!

To *achieve* beauty, a lady needs her beauty or make-up kit. She also needs flashy clothes and shoes. Then she has to get a number of *artificials:* — hair, fingernails, toenails and even breasts (if hers happen to be the size of table tennis balls).

Since the face is the *public relations manager* of the lady's body, that is where the effort to achieve beauty should commence and concentrate on To do this in conformity with modern fads, a lady must carefully scrape off her eyebrows. Then, she should use her black eyelid pencil to draw a very visible but tiny black line where the eyebrows used to be. She must ensure that the line achieves its desired effect - to make the lady appear like a Mongolian puppet!

Farther down the face, the lips should be vigorously painted with lipstick. So thick must the layer of lipstick be (colour depends on the *painter*) that the lady should be sighted from half a kilometre away.

The entire face should be thoroughly massaged and powdered. Then, what they call *rosy-cheeks* should be used to paint the cheek and the portion of the face between the pencil-line (former eyebrows) and the eyes. Again, the choice of colours of the *rosy-cheeks* depends on the user. The important thing is to end up looking like an enthusiastic participant in the Indian festival of colours or like an *Ekpo masquerade* from the Akwa Ibom area of Nigeria.

When the face has been fully taken care of, the hair has to be the next target. A lady's hair, it is said, is her source of beauty. A trip to the hairdresser is therefore essential. There, her hair is either *permed* or *jelly curled*. These may entail a two-hour period of excruciating heat and pain under the drier. But, that's a small price to pay for beauty!

Alternatively, the lady can weave her hair (not the traditional style) in the Bob Marley or Rastafarian way. This can be *carried* for three months. It saves time and money. That the hair might be full of dandruff and possibly be stinking in this period, doesn't really matter.

A lady ought to know that in the honourable quest for beauty, the hairstyle she chooses might not necessarily be because it best suits her, but because that is what is in vogue. Should the style make her look like an owl, why should she bother? That is what beauty is all about.

Clothes maketh a woman. This as an unforgettable maxim in beauty circles. A lady must be quite fastidious over the sort of cloth she wears. That is why it must take her no less than three hours to dress up for any occasion. In fashion-conscious Africa, ladies know that the more weird a dress looks, the better for the wearer and her wonderful designer! Like a virus, that weird style would be the *vogue* in town sooner than later. That the dress happens to turn a normal human being who wears it into an *unidentified walking object (UWO)* should not bother the lady. Afterall, the beauty of being beautiful is to do the outlandish. If the cloth is not enough to sew what the lady really desires, she should settle for something tremendously short, barely covering her underwear. This is the wonderful style called *mini*. The only piece of advice to the wearer is that if she happens to be in Nairobi, Kenya's capital city, she must not go near a place called Luthuli Avenue. Over there, some self-anointed guardians of public morality and their legion of thugs and miscreants might pounce on, and forcefully relieve the lady of her mini and underwear, thus exposing her *hidden agenda!*

As a rule, all clothes and dresses must be dry-cleaned, even handkerchiefs. A nice and romantic lady should not destroy her manicured fingernails washing clothes!

After the dress, shoes are the next in the precious order of importance. Shoes must be worn to match the dress. Same with handbags. The only rule about shoes is that the higher they are, the better. They must be such that they make a lady walk in distorted strides, as if she is walking on top of a rocky mountain.

The type of body cream a lady uses makes or mars her beauty. A truly beautiful African lady is one whose skin looks like that of a European. Consequently, the creams which should be used are those that must bleach away the dark skin the African lady was born with. She must be seen to be *yellow*. If the lady was born fair, that's a bonus for it would be easier to bleach into the white skin from the light body colour. On this score, the likes of Yaya Jameh, the Gambian President who decreed that bleaching is punishable by law, do not know that they are trampling on the fundamental human cum skin rights our dear sisters of the *dark* continent possess. They need serious prayers for divine forgiveness.

The only little snag about bleaching is that after some months or years, the lady shall notice the emergence of some dark patches all over her body, especially the neck, legs and thighs. But, these do not mean much. It is better to look beautiful with those patches than look ugly without them. In any case, what are long skirts, flowing gowns and wrappers for? They should be enough to cover the legs which those militant dark spots love to attack.

A beautiful lady has to generously spray her body, at regular intervals, with assorted perfumes. The armpits (even after using deodorants) should have their perfume. So should the wrists, ears, neck and the rest of the body. All are aimed at making a lady stay fresh and beautiful.

Weight-watching is equally important. The books on beauty tips have to be bought as soon as they are published in order to learn the latest ways to stay trim. But, reading those books should be another thing altogether!

A lady who observes all these shall certainly look beautiful. She will be the toast of all men!

Agelessness

It remains a puzzle why ladies all over the world generally hide their age. Amongst African ladies, the greater puzzle is the intensity and obsession with which they make sure men never get to know how old they really are. Where it is mandatory to disclose their age, they either devalue it like most African currencies, or simply put down *adult* on spaces provided for age.

Irony steps in here. When they are between 18 and 24 years, ladies tell their age with glee. They also tell their achievements - like having graduated from the university at 18 or 20 and bagging a postgraduate degree at 21. Thereafter, an eclipse overshadows their age.

Again, another irony. An African lady must never forget to celebrate her birthday. Such occasions are the *grand slams* of the year. Gifts are expected. Felicitations freely flow. There is so much to eat and drink. The only taboo is to try and unravel her age. Such questions *spoil her day!*

At weddings, a lady's age is cleverly hidden. But a man's age is told as a matter of routine. Since hers is shrouded in mystery, what a fortunate audience may hear is that *she was born when her mates were born.* Beyond that, the *age* door is firmly shut.

Honestly, a respectable lady should not waste her time on such trivialities as age. African men often go for the shadows. Instead of assessing a lady by her worth, they attach more importance to extraneous factors as age. A lady must therefore conceal her age. For her, the magical age should be 21. After several years, she could move to 24. Then, she is free to stay there for as long as she wishes. Afterall, this is a free world!

Any constant reference to age must be brushed aside with ignominy. Life is too short and sweet to be burdened with such nonsense. Two sisters, both elderly, nearly fought over this age business in public. Trouble started when the older sister found it nauseating that her younger sister had formed the bad habit of introducing her as *my elder sister* at all gatherings. She consequently handed down an order to be introduced just as *my sister*. Why? Because she knew that the younger one was not doing so out of respect, but just to express how young she was to the public, and dismiss her elder sister as an *old hag!*

The essence of African womanhood is to stay young. Fortunately, there are technological gadgets in this modern era which aid this ambition. There are beauty clinics to ensure that the aged look like today's news!

Agelessness is a good sport. Every lady should engage in it. Men are thrilled by it. The lady who allows herself to look as old as she really is, or tells her age, is destined to be tagged an *old cargo* even by older women and men! The best option is to stay young, fresh and ageless!!

Attitude Towards Marriage

Marriage and related issues do not qualify for any space on the personal agenda of any respectable lady. A lady has to be so preoccupied with so many other things that garnish life to have time for such a nuisance as marriage. Besides, the marriage institution imposes tremendous cultural inhibitions on ladies that no reasonable lady should contemplate surrendering her freedom for any reason at all, to it.

To belong to the esoteric league of ladies is never to be *ready or ripe* for marriage. Marriage, to the lady, is something that should not be *rushed into*; it is a life-long commitment that requires years of hard thinking and careful planning. Moreover, African men are irretrievable amateurs on how to treat a lady. So, the rational thing to do is for the lady to be wary of marriage until *Mr Right* comes along.

A lady therefore reserves the right to declare her unreadiness for marriage despite the fact that no proposal to that effect has been made. It will just be a warning to men!

Marriage, nonetheless, should not be a complete taboo to a modern lady. It is something she can and should discuss more passionately without really getting involved in it. It is from such discussions that what a man must possess before he qualifies as Mr Right are amply stated and debated. Here are some of the requirements to be satisfied before a man can be considered as *Mr. Right:*

Wealth: Mr Right has to be considerably wealthy. Being able to provide the traditional *three square meals* a day is not enough. He must have a steady (not necessarily visible source) income. How that income is made is immaterial. The important thing is that money should keep piling up in the man's vault. He has to live in a posh house and drive the latest car from Japan or Germany. If he is a man known all over the elite circles in town, that's a big plus!

Education: Mr Right does not have to be well read. A basic education is sufficient, even if it stopped at the primary level. He only has to be literate enough to speak the English language, or bulldoze his way through it, without embarrassing the lady in front of her friends. These days, education without wealth might well be called illiteracy!

Physical features: Gone are the days when being handsome was a prominent determinant in who the eventual bridegroom should be. What should matter is how *good looking* the would-be bridegroom's pocket is. That he is partially deformed, a near dwarf, seriously pot-bellied or barely distinguishable from a dragon does not count much. The definition of an ugly man is he who is poor!

Family background: This should not also matter much. The person being married is the bridegroom, not his family. In any case, the modern lady has to put a great distance between her husband and his family once they are married.

General: The man must be *loving and caring* and should show both! These are measured by the number of expensive things he buys for the lady, how often he buys her tickets for holidays abroad and how much (and often) liquid cash he gives her. The man should throw away his manly pride and help out with the regular chores at home.
    Even with these requirements a lady must be careful about getting married. She has a more rollicking life awaiting her outside a matrimonial home!

Post script. When all things fail and the lady appears to be finding it difficult to get Mr Right, she must settle for Mr Available. Afterall, one man is just like another!

Expected Courtesies

If a lady comports herself at all times, then she certainly is entitled to some courtesies from the male folk.

Unfortunately, many African men are stark ignorant about the courtesies their ladies deserve. Despite the fact that they constantly watch Western movies and see how European and American ladies are treated by their men, some of them still think that ladies are like pieces of furniture to be handled as their owner pleases.

A modern African lady should not allow herself to be so treated. Should her man or any man for that matter behave in an unbecoming manner, he should be cut down to size without delay. Thus, when expected courtesies are not carried out by men, decent ladies should demand for them. That is part of what being a lady is all about.

Luncheon courtesies:

As soon as she steps into the venue for a luncheon, a lady deserves to be excitedly welcomed by her host (forget hostess for now).

"I'm highly honoured that you found time to come, Sheila."

"It's my pleasure."

"*By Jove!* You look stunningly beautiful in your most elegant dress."

"Oh, thanks."

"(In a whisper) Your hairdresser certainly knows her trade. This is how a lady's hair should look."

"Oh, thank you very much," she replies, giggling as she does so.

The next phase of the courtesy comes when the guests are to be invited to the table. The announcer must be careful at this point. The standard thing to say is: " Ladies and gentlemen, lunch is served. May I invite the ladies to............"

This is what is called *ladies first*. Courtesy demands that ladies should go for the meal first. The idea is that if men with their ravenous appetite and pot-bellies are allowed to pounce on the food, the poor ladies shall go home hungry. Never mind that after *ladies first*, there is hardly a *last* for men as all the choice delicacies will have vanished onto the ladies' plates!

Other courtesies

- If, at a gathering, there are few seats for the guests, men, being the gentle men they are expected to be, should get up for their more delicate ladies to sit down; it may not matter that the man surrendering his seat is fit to be the lady's grandfather.

- A man is supposed to open the car's door for the lady to step inside, shut it, before walking round to his own seat.

- In a man's shop, a lady is expected to buy things at a cheaper price. That is the price the shop owner has to pay for the lady's charm and smiles.

- A taxi ought to take a lady to wherever her destination is, irrespective of how inconvenient that shall be to other male passengers who boarded the taxi before her; that is, in countries where two or more people board a taxi at the same time.
- When a lady is making a call at a public phone (even private telephones), she should spend as much time as she wants. Men, as gentle as ever, can always wait.
- When a lady is taken out for lunch, she should be cajoled to try this and that item on the menu, and wash everything down with vintage wine. Even when she declares that *I'm full* in that tender voice, she should be persuaded to eat a little more.
- If a lady's car breaks down or she has a flat tyre, a proper gentleman should pull over and help her repair the damage irrespective of the fact that she would hardly do the same if the situation were reversed.
- Ladies must not be left to stand in the sun or rain. Gentlemen with cars should give them a ride. That ladies hardly give men a ride is also irrelevant.
- In offices, ladies should be given the less demanding tasks. Even the little they have should be taken away from them and given to the overloaded donkeys called men.
- A lady must not be rushed into dressing up for an occasion, although she might have already caused a one-hour delay for whatever was planned.
- Harsh words and insults should not be rained on a lady. But if she happens to haul insults at a man, he should take them *like a man*.
- A man should not refuse a lady's request except under extreme circumstances, otherwise he should he declared a *mean* person.

Taxi Lessons
(in countries where two or more persons can share a taxi)

Lesson 1 : A confident lady should always remember that she is paying for the ride. The taxi driver therefore has to perform his function to her satisfaction. Anything less should be condemned. And the driver has to be reminded that he is a *common driver,* should he get swollen-headed and nasty.

Lesson 2 : Taxi drivers are largely illiterate. Therefore a lady has to talk to them in Queen's English. If the poor fellow needs an interpreter to understand her, that's his problem.

Lesson 3 : The comfort of other passengers in the taxi has to be secondary. A lady does not have to emerge from a taxi looking scruffy.

Lesson 4 : The choice position in a taxi is the front seat. If the lady cannot get it, she should wait for the next taxi. But if she is in a hurry, she may *manage* with the back seat.

Lesson 5 : A lady should insist on sitting by the window side so that she can manipulate it at will. Sitting in the middle will give her a sense of being clustered, and her dress might get creased beyond tolerable limits.

Lesson 6 : While sitting by the window, a lady should wind up the glass in the interest of her hair. The inflow of wind destroys the beauty of her hair. That other poor passengers may feel suffocated should not be her problem.

Lesson 7 : When two friendly ladies are in a taxi, they should feel free to chat, laugh and jab at each other. They have no business talking in low tones and the other passengers have no business complaining about being disturbed.

Lesson 8 : A lady should not disembark until she gets to her doorstep. No one has any right to plead with her to alight thirty metres to her house so that the rest can avoid a terrible traffic hold-up in front of them.

Lesson 9 : If she chooses, she may produce a $100 bill for a trip that requires only 50 cents. Should the driver protest that he has no *change*, he has to be ignored. She should tell him off if he tries to be nasty. A lady has to be firm over such matters.

Lesson 10 : If a taxi driver tries to demonstrate his stubbornness, a no-nonsense lady should threaten to *deal with him*. She should drop a few names that will convince the driver that she has the *right connections to finish him*.

Lesson 11 : If any passenger decides to take sides with the driver should an argument ensue, the lady should also tell him off. He must be told to *mind your own business*. If it's another lady, she should look at her scornfully and hiss.

Lesson 12 : As a rule, a lady should not tell a taxi driver where exactly she is going. She should give a vague destination. When she gets to where the driver thinks she's going, she should tell him to go left, then right, then go straight and turn left again. If he protests, she must tongue-lash him thoroughly. If he refuses to go any farther, the lady can get down and walk away. No payment. He has not fulfilled his part of the bargain, so why pay him? Not being exact about destinations is another way of saving money on a trip!

Accepting A Ride

When it comes to getting a ride, ladies have an overwhelming advantage over men. While a man who genuinely needs a ride hardly gets it, a lady who hardly needs it is appealed to, to accept it. Even when she initially bluffs whoever stops to give her a ride, she is still cajoled to accept it.

Although a lady may want a ride, she has to be very selective in the choice of car she hops into. It's no use seeking a ride in a car whose worth is no more than the cost of the lady's dress and bangles! Or those that are so dilapidated that after a ride in them one has to go for some medication for joint pains and headache. The cars which a decent lady should go for are the very flashy ones. These are the state-of-the-art cars which dazzle the eyes and offer tremendous comfort.

A lady who needs a ride must not stand with the crowd. She has to move some metres away. As the car approaches, she has to establish an eye contact with the driver. A wink might do the trick!

Should the driver fail to notice this, the lady should stick out her hand a little and flag down the car. If he doesn't stop, a torrent of abuses and curses on the driver, but mumbled to herself, shall be appropriate. Yes, for why should anyone fail to offer a decent lady a *lift*?

When a car stops to give the lady a *lift*, she must not under any circumstance rush for it. Indeed, the real thing to do is to look the other way and pretend not to have noticed the car. The lady should allow those beside her to inform her that a car has stopped for her. Or, she should let the driver reverse and stop just where she is standing.

Even then, a lady with a measure of dignity should not hurry into the car, especially if she did not flag it down. The thing to do is to allow the driver to beckon to her. Then, she should walk majestically to the car, stop beside the window, switch on her charm and ask a *may I help you* rhetorical question in a most tender voice!

"Care for a ride?" the self-adjudged lucky man asks, beaming his tooth-paste smile.
"It depends on where you are going."
"Where are you going?"
"Towards the new post office."
"Fine, hop in."
Before a lady steps into the car, she needs to cast an I-do-not-belong-to-your-class glance at the people near her. It is necessary for a lady to show the other people that there is something special about her!

When does a lady need a *lift*? It depends. On what? That also depends. The general rule however is that a lady needs a lift when she is actually in no hurry to go to her destination; she has money but does not want to spend it on taxi fare; and is seeking for some fun.

Once a lady is inside the car, only a few men would resist the urge to *chat her up*. So, any lady looking for a ride has to be ready with her answers.

Scenario 1 : When a lady is out for fun

"*Hi*, pretty lady, you look stunning in that dress (a lie). From where did you buy it?"

"London, last summer (she blushes)."

"You sure have *taste*. What's your name? I'm Taiwo."

"Bisi is the name (a lie of course). Nice to meet you."

"Nice to meet you too. If you don't mind, may I have the privilege of buying you a drink if you are not in a hurry."

"(Looks at her wrist-watch for effect) I wouldn't mind, Yomi."

"No, I'm Taiwo, Bisi."

"Sorry, Taiwo. I have an uncle called Yomi whom I'm very fond of, that's why I call his name all the time (a lie)."

"Oh yeah!"

"Sure. We can go for the drink but we must hurry up. I've got an appointment to catch."

That's one appointment she'll never *catch*!

Scenario 2 : When a lady cares about her dignity
"*Hi*, pretty lady, you look stunning in that dress, from where did you buy it?"

"In one of the boutiques down town, thanks."

"You sure have *taste*. What's your name? I'm Taiwo."

"Bisi (truth or lie)."

"Nice to meet you."

"Nice to meet you, too."

"May I have the privilege to buy you a drink?"

"No, thanks."

"Maybe next time?"

"Yes, maybe."

"When exactly?"

"Please mind your driving, we might bump into something, you know."

"Ah! Don't worry. How do I see you again? Here's my business card."

"Thanks, I shall phone you. Kindly drop me behind that blue Volkswagen. Thanks for the ride."

"My pleasure. I shall be expecting your call."

"Please do."

The card is torn and thrown in the nearest waste paper basket, and the man's name forgotten!

Post script: *The only danger in accepting a ride from complete strangers is that one might end up with armed bandits or a rapist!*

What To Read; What To Watch

A woman who is serious about being a lady has to be mindful of what materials she reads and the movies or television programmes she watches. Reading or watching the wrong things pollutes the mind and threatens the beauty and quality of being a lady.

The general golden rule is that a thoughtful lady should spend more time and money looking after herself than on what to read or watch. Put in the ordinary man's language, a lady has to be quite lazy about reading, and should hardly find time for some *watching* - unless she is watching herself in the mirror!

If a lady must read however, top on her reading list should be the love-romance stories. The *Mills and Boon* series or the *Denise Robbins* novels come in handy. Indeed, these are like standard texts for budding African ladies. African female writers are yet to *mature* and write for the delicate and exquisite tastes of their female folk. Nonetheless, some female writers, like Helen Ovbiagele of Nigeria who wrote the enchanting *Evbu my Love*, at times walk their way into the modern ladies' reading list. Generally, foreign female authors who write close to fantasies are the darling of African ladies.

Next to the love-romance materials, a lady has to be well acquainted with the gossip magazines. These thrill the reader, for they unearth the intimate and secret lives of celebrities, especially women.

Fashion comes next. A lady's ultimate business is to look good and attractive. Although she knows what to do to look beautiful, she needs to read and learn how to even look more beautiful - what to wear, how and when to wear them, et cetera. In fact, cartoons are not that important, but ladies may need them to enliven the spirit.

As for the television, it is necessary to the extent that the lady can watch soap operas. Again, this is understandable in the sense that these soaps dwell on love and romance as their themes.

To keep her sanity, a lady has to avoid newspapers and news magazines like the plague. What business does a lady have with what the Chinese students and their authorities did at Beijing's Tianamen Square in June, 1989? Of what relevance are the 1989 events in Eastern Europe or the ousting and execution of the former Romanian leader, Nicolae Ceacescu, to the African lady? And Archbishop Desmond Tutu, does he know anything about fashion and beauty to arrest the attention of African ladies? People like the flamboyant Winnie-Madikizela Mandela make more sense to read about and watch, not because of her role in the anti-apartheid struggle or her contributions in post-apartheid South Africa, but because of her fashionable apparels and hairdo!

If, for any reason, a lady should find herself with a newspaper, she should go straight to the fashion and woman pages, read the horoscope column and fling the thing away! If there is an apparent contradiction in the facts that a lady who abhors reading newspapers also went through schools where she had to read text books, the explanation is not hard to come by: it was necessary to read those boring textbooks in order to pass examinations. Newspapers and similar materials have no such utilitarian content.

Out For Lunch

Only an incredibly disgusting lady should reject a lunch offer from a man, especially if he is known to her. Invariably, such a lady must either be a *born-again* Christian or a Muslim fundamentalist who feels it is a sin against God to be seen with a man, what is more, going out with him for lunch in a restaurant.

A modern lady must rely on the number of times she is invited for lunch as part of her criteria for measuring her standing amongst the male folk. Should she be totally ignored, something must be fundamentally wrong. The more she gets such invitations, the stronger the evidence that she is a *hot cake* among men.

A respectable lady never solicits for lunch. But it is permissible for her to drop intelligent hints that she wouldn't reject it if offered. How she does this depends on the circumstances. No hard rules about it.

African men are very vain people. They are prepared to sell their birthright if only to impress ladies. This is something a lady must always bear in mind whenever she is offered lunch. Chances are that the man would also offer her the choice of the venue for the lunch. Here, a decent lady should pretend she has never heard of the word *caution*, and go for the best restaurant or hotel. The man, feeling that his prestige is at stake, is more likely to say, *that's a wonderful choice, let's go!*

Once at the lunch venue, a lady has to pretend to be very familiar with the environment. On no account should the man be allowed to suspect that the lady is just having her first experience in such an exquisite environment. But, he must be allowed to do most of the talking. Nothing would boost his ego as much so being seen to be in charge of affairs.

Lunch etiquette demands that a lady must not be modest in whatever she would order. Wine? She should go for the vintage stuff. Food? Place an order for the most exotic and expensive. If the menu is written in French or German, and the meaning is uncertain, the lady should go for that which appears most complex. Alternatively, she could keep the waiter for ten minutes, during which time a trip across the dishes would have been made, their contents questioned and explained, and a combination of two or more of the food items made in one order! That is the beauty of lunch - when a man is paying for it.

When the food finally arrives, the lady should ask for *chicken* if the plate has beef. When the *chicken part* is brought, the lady can make one of those *if you don't mind* apologies to the man and proceed to call for some fish! Then, a general complaint about too much or too little pepper or salt or that the food is just *flat*, may follow.

Should the man's food arrive first, one of those *may I please*, which sound more like an order, should be said so that the lady can eat out of the dish. Should hers come first, she doesn't have to wait for his to be served before she starts eating. This is against table manners (although he would wait if his came first). So, with a barely audible *oh, I'm starving*, the lady should pounce on the dish. Then, after eating no more than a small portion of it, she should, again barely audibly, declare that *oh, I'm so full*. A lady should not be seen to eat too much - at a time!

While lunch is going on, occasional trips to the man's plate to scavenge for meat and all that, is permissible. The man will only be too happy with such a development. He might even mistake it for affection or love as African men readily conclude if a lady does as little as smile at them.

After the meal, a lady who is used to being taken out for lunch should call for an extra glass of wine et cetera. A little coyish smile at the man, followed by a *hope you don't mind* said in a romantic voice, should earn her the man's permission to go ahead.

The bill? That should not be the lady's concern. Being taken out for lunch does not mean that she is responsible for the bill or part of it, or more importantly, that she should be mindful of what to order for, in order to keep the bill within reasonable limits. The maxim is that if a man does not have enough money, he has no business taking a lady out for lunch or dinner.

After lunch, a lady should quickly express her readiness to leave in order to catch up with another appointment. This is very important for African men often feel that buying a lady lunch is all they need to deliver their *manifesto* to her; or that buying lunch gives them a measure of authority over the lady.

One more thing; a lady who cherishes her pride must not say thank you after the lunch. The man should do it to her, for joining him for a lunch is a big favour. And when he does acknowledge this by saying *so nice of you to have joined me for lunch*, a complete lady should just smile and murmur *you're welcome!*

Going Shopping

Men go to the market to *buy a few things*; ladies go *shopping*.

Shopping is a more dignified way of going to make purchases. It shows that the purchaser knows exactly what to buy, where to buy them, at what price and how to make a distinction between the real and fake products displayed for purchasing. That is a lady's approach to the art of buying things.

For a lady, there is a ritual about going shopping. A level-headed lady does not make an impromptu shopping. If she should be compelled to make a few purchases before her normal shopping time, then that act is ordinarily called *going to the market*. Forget that she might buy more things in this process than when she does the real shopping.

A lady therefore has to plan her shopping in advance. Better, if her plan remains a secret. Where a lady does her shopping is largely a personal affair. The only person to whom the venue of the shopping should be made known to is her very close and trusted friend. This is absolutely important for practically everything a decent African lady wears has to be bought from Europe or America! That *Europe* might be beside Tinubu Square in Lagos or Gikomba Sunshine Boutique in Nairobi. It could even be an area where smuggled goods or second-hand dresses are sold at give-away prices. If the dress is bought from such a place for instance, it is quickly sent to the dry-cleaners, reclaimed and baptised a *bought-from-London dress!* Alternatively, the smart lady should declare that her auntie, boyfriend or colleague bought it for her in Paris.

It is therefore advisable for a lady to do her shopping alone.

To go for shopping, a lady needs a lot of energy. As a rule, she must not walk into a shop, buy whatever she is interested in and head for home. No. Shopping is more exciting when the lady goes round the market or shopping centre looking for what she can find everywhere! If the item is a pin, several shops have to be visited to eliminate the possibility of buying a fake pin!

Then, there is the fastidious aspect of shopping. If a headdress is to be bought, then the lady must search for one that meets a motley of criteria. If it is of the desired quality, it may be disqualified on the grounds of colour. If the colour is alright, then the designs might not be attractive. If everything about the material is fine, it can still be rejected on the grounds that the lady needs to move around to see if she could find something better. Then she takes note of the shop for she may have to go back there eventually.

Then, there is the price factor. A lady doing shopping should not accept whatever price she is told the item costs. Haggling is something she has to be quite adept at doing. Once the price is announced by the seller, a lady on shopping has to slash it by 80%. Then she begins to concede at the rate of 5 per cent until she can concede no more. At the end of the session, the lady may find it wise to abandon the material because she cannot afford to pay $10 for it, unless the seller is prepared to accept $9.50. But, had she gone with a man who is sponsoring the shopping, she would pick up the same material for $20 and comment that *it's so cheap!*

After haggling from shop to shop for two hours or more, and making sure that there are no better designs, colours and quality of the item to be purchased, the lady shopper might decide to go back to the first shop she entered at the beginning of the shopping to buy the item.

At times, it might be expedient for the lady to temporarily forget what she had come to shop for, and engage in some window-shopping. While doing this, haggling and searching for the best price for what she has no intention of buying, would be perfectly in order.

The beauty and essence of shopping is that so much time is devoted to buying so little. A lady who is extremely exhausted after a shopping session might have the following on her shopping list:

Deodorant :   *Bought.*
Pants :   *The right colours not seen.*
Shoes: *Found where to buy them next time.*
Cloth: *Two metres bought; shall go back for two more.*
Nail polish :   *Very expensive; better to buy from the kiosk near home.*

A lady whose purchases exceed the items listed above did not go shopping - *she went to the market!*

Being Chased

Very few things delight a perfect African lady as much as having men run after her, professing their love in what is called the *chasing* game.

Consequently, a lady looks forward to being chased, not only by serious-minded, potential lovers, but by those whose intentions may not be so noble. To have men struggle to win her over is part of the things that keep a lady *alive and kicking*. What better way is there for a lady to boast of her charm than for her to fill friends with stories about how Prince X and Dr. T *have been all over me in the last couple of days!*

Moreover, a self-confident lady should know that her type is hard to find and get. Nice, decent ladies are rare. A man must therefore sweat it out in order to find one.

The chasing game is a very slippery affair. It is also a business where, to make a point, one must appear to be talking backwards - intentions are never made directly. If a man should walk up to a lady and tell her he wishes that they become lovers, a respectable lady should at best ignore him and walk away. Otherwise, a bit of tongue-lashing would be an appropriate response.

To chase a lady in a way she would appreciate, the chaser must do a great deal of stalking - just like what a cat does when it sees a rat that might make a delicious dinner. The chaser must also possess the right credentials - a good job, education, social status and wealth. A pauper has no business chasing a lady.

Ladies are quite enthralled by the preliminaries of the chasing game and are more responsive when they are embarked upon in style. A lady expects (and the chaser ought to know) the man to begin the ritual by demonstrating that he is a nice person who deserves a chance to show just how nice he is.

A man should send specially selected cards that indicate his intentions. He should offer the lady a ride to and from work, invite her for lunch or an outing et cetera. But once he begins to do these, an intelligent lady should take the cue and tell him straightaway that she is not interested in whatever he is after. Normally, men don't give up once they are told that. Indeed, they see it as a form of a greenlight to go ahead with whatever they intend to do.

But a lady who is being chased and who knows her worth should stick to her guns and repeatedly show that she is not ready for an affair. A quick indication of readiness that is devoid of pretences makes an African lady feel cheap and unsophisticated!

What a wise lady should do at this point is to do everything to keep him at bay. The man can be told to visit her when she knows she'll not be at home or in the office. She can promise to visit him when she knows she wouldn't. She may promise to go to a party with him and back out at the last minute - with apparent sincere apologies.

All these are supposed to increase a lady's worth. When a man eventually tells a lady about a possible relationship, she should plead for time - weeks or months - to consider the request, although she might be ready with the reply right there.

Incidentally and interestingly, a lady might initiate the process of being chased. Should she see a man worthy of her love, she could encourage him to chase her by giving him the right signals that she could be available!

The essence of being chased is not the aftermath - agreeing to be lovers or not - but to show that a lady is a woman of honour and prestige who has to be systematically wooed and appealed to before a request is granted. Should she sidetrack the chasing game, the African man could just mistake her honesty and sincerity for being gullible and cheap.

When To Hiss

It isn't exactly polite for a glamorous lady to be seen hissing like a spitting cobra. But it pays her to hiss from time to time. Instead of engaging herself in verbal warfare against someone - a thing a decent lady should have no time and energy for - she should do the quickest thing to dismiss a potential adversary: Hiss!

Hissing, nonetheless, loses its effect when it is not done properly. A hiss that comes and goes in a flash achieves quite little. The proper way to do it is to prolong it and let the other person go raving mad. In addition, the lady has to seriously distort her face in such a way as to indicate condescension or slight. Then she should swing her head from one side to another, eyes partially or fully closed, as the protracted hissing goes on.

A variety of reasons can compel a lady to hiss. Here are some of them.

- When another lady, dressed quite sophisticatedly, walks past in a way as to confer some importance and class on herself. A hiss is appropriate here to protest such a display of arrogance and vanity.
- When a lady is in the house and another woman steps in, looking for her (original lady's) boyfriend. The door should be slammed in her face, accompanied by a hiss.
- When another lady is on phone, asking to speak to the lady's boyfriend. The lady should warn her not to attempt making such phone calls, furiously drop the receiver and hiss.
- When a lady is told by her boss to work harder or when whatever she has done is criticised and regarded as below standard. A hiss here would be a subtle way to protest the boss' fastidiousness.
- When, inside a bus or *matatu*, a man tries to be friendly by initiating a conversation. A hiss at this point should be a *polite* way of telling him to shut up!
- When an unsolicited ride is offered and the lady is uninterested. If the man persists, a hiss should be an initial warning for him *to buzz off*.

- In the course of a gossip session, a hiss here and there would be appropriate to embellish the story.
- When a lady is sulking.
- When a lady intends to declare her hostility.
- When a lady wants to let others around her know that she is not in their class, especially if they reject her wise suggestions or opinions.
- When something nice happens. A hiss would be a way of saying *I knew it would happen!*

Whatever the situation, a lady should feel free to hiss. If this does not go down well with people around her, too bad. The hallmark of being a respectable lady is to be fiercely independent and assertive. A hiss just drives the point home.

Going For A Weekend

Old-fashioned ladies worry and work themselves into a frenzy over what to take along for a weekend. They don't seem to know what they'll need. They are so enslaved by the fear of *bothering* their host or hostess that they end up travelling with enough luggage for a three-month vacation.

Modern ladies are not so fettered by such out-moded conventions and considerations. A weekend luggage should not be more than a small travelling bag that could be hung on the shoulder and carried with the greatest ease.

The contents of such a bag depend on the person and place of visit. But the general rule is that the make-up kit must be there. If the visit is to an old girlfriend or colleague, a few dresses and sundry items would be sufficient. The lady can always *manage* with her hostess's. It should be easy for the visiting lady to feign forgetfulness: *Oh my Gad, why did I forget the blouse I wanted to wear to the party? Imagine, I put it on the bed and just forgot the damn thing!* Upon hearing her screaming and cursing, the hostess, kind-hearted as she is, should readily produce an alternative with a plea to her guest to *manage with this*. In this way, the problem of a dress is solved. Thereafter, the lady might plead with her hostess to *let me go and dry-clean the stuff before giving it back to you*. That dress might not be returned!

If the visit is to an auntie who never misses attending her Sunday church service, going with a small Bible may be a wise decision. Madam Auntie won't have to bore her guest with spiritual talk for the Bible would be a sure sign that her *little niece* (no matter how old and big the lady is) has not sold her soul to the devil!

If the visit is to the lady's parents (which rarely happens these days when all ladies swear they can *take care* of themselves, only to start screaming *mummy, daddy* over a minor headache), then the idea of going with a bag might be ruled out completely. Afterall, mummy's dresses, shoes and jewelry are there to wear, although the lady should first condemn them as being no longer in vogue! She should also try out her older sister's dresses and so on.

If the visit is to a boyfriend, one item is a must for the handbag: a little mallet. That could be her offence or defence weapon. If the man is a *ladies' man*, chances are that a member of his harem might also visit that weekend. The mallet could be a handy weapon to *chase dem krazy gals out of the house.* Or a lady may find it quite useful if the intruder is one of those *Lagos, Accra or Harare gals* who derive immense pleasure from stampeding *real madams* out of the house!

A first weekend visit to a boyfriend imposes restrictions on a lady; like how to take two tea-spoonfuls of rice and proclaim that she has had more than enough to eat! It should also be an opportunity for the lady to try out her pet theories about men — like her belief that nothing stops a lady from lying down in bed while her man prepares and serves her breakfast there!

Talking Big

Talking big is an essential ingredient of being an African lady. It adds glamour to her life. It bestows a measure of respect, amazement and pride on her. Without it, her colleagues and acquaintances would most likely disregard her views. And when there is a party, picnic or jamboree to attend, no one would remember to include her name on the guest list.

The most fertile issue on which to talk big is travelling. African ladies give the impression that they tend to be prone to developing cancer when they travel within their continent. So, they generally do not like travelling in their immediate environment. Those who manage to do so have indeed not achieved anything. They are no more than *local champions.*

Once, a contestant in a beauty pageant in Nigeria told the compere that her hobby included travelling. When asked where she had visited, she effortlessly reeled off the names of several cities in Nigeria! She was booed off the stage! *She was no lady!!*

Real ladies must have travelled across the globe. Summer must have been spent in Liechtenstein; winter, with the happy Eskimos of Greenland; spring, in Kualar Lumpur and autumn in Laos. Then on her way back home, she must have made a stop-over in Monaco! These relatively unknown places imply that she has been to the known parts of the world. And the implication is clear: a lady who boasts of travelling to places like London and New York will immediately be recognised as a novice in the travelling business. African ladies have reduced USA and Britain to pedestrian spots!

A lady cannot authoritatively lay claims to being *somebody* until she has attended one of those ubiquitously exclusive parties in town. Such are the places where only the *very cream of the society* are seen . For a lady to have had an opportunity to attend such parties, it must mean that *she has arrived,* socially. So would her listeners be made to believe.

Talking big means living big too, or pretending to be doing so. A lady is one who works as a junior secretary but lives like a permanent secretary. Please don't ask her how she manages to live above her means. Such a question would be considered an insult.

A lady's dresses, shoes, trinkets et cetera, must all be quite expensive and of the finest quality. When asked the price of whatever she puts on, adding $50 to the real value is quite in order. Indeed, this would be considered very modest. Bolder ladies feel free to inflate the price by as much as $200. Insisting that all clothes were specially designed for her is also in order.

Talking big has more credibility if a lady owns a car. If not, taxies are the next best alternative. If she happens to be travelling by bus (real ladies don't do that, trust them!), she must pray that no one recognises her. A lady with class must show that she is *not used to hard life*.

When dresses and jewelry are brought to her office, Miss Big Talker just has to make huge purchases in order to sustain her prestige. Those who don't have this habit of patronising office sales are never reckoned with in fashion circles. If it means buying the material on credit, the lady has to do so. If it means starving at home, she also has to do it, afterall no one would ever know about the starvation.

If name-dropping is not done with zeal, a lady cannot be said to be in the *big league*, and cannot talk big. She must have an impressive list of boyfriends - current, retired and even *envisaged!* These are high-profile boyfriends whose names should be dropped as casually as possible, when and where the dropping would make the greatest impact.

A lady should be able to have a clear idea of what whoever shall eventually marry her should be. Her vision should be that of a man who has virtually achieved all there is to achieve in his field. He must be rich and handsome, and an active member of the exclusive *Amedollar club*, the fictitious *American dollar club* created by the late Nigerian writer, Ken Saro-Wiwa, in his television series entitled *Mr B*. Besides, *the lucky man* should be enlightened enough to treat the lady as his equal, no less. There is no way a lady big-talker could condescend to marry a lesser personality. When it comes to marrying a man of moderate quality, Miss Big Talker's love ceases to be blind.

How To Speak

When it comes to speaking the English language, men are no match for ladies. Men, unlike ladies, have so battered their voice boxes with bouts of *booze*, spirits and cigarettes that they have lost that smoothness with which ladies pronounce words when they speak.

A lady, therefore, has to speak the English language with an arresting fluidity, and with a voice so sonorous that birds would hide themselves in shame.

Talking about speaking generally (not necessarily the English language) a lady must be careful not to be vulgar. Men are the incurable users of all foul and gutter language. The only time it may be permissible for a lady to go vulgar in her choice of words is when she is amongst other ladies (her intimate friends of course) and in private. In public, a lady should twitch in apparent agony or show utter disgust upon hearing vulgar words being spoken. It is unimaginable therefore that she would say those words herself.

Back to English which is the language of communication in many parts of Africa. For a lady to be recognised as being in the league of good speakers of the language, her elocution must be beyond reproach. Phonetics is the name of the game, so she has to be able to pronounce English words in such a soothing way that the Queen of England should be impressed.

When a lady is speaking in a public place like her office, the phonetical magic should be switched on to its highest pitch. But in the privacy of her room, she can afford to speak more naturally!

The idea of the phonetical gymnastics is to demonstrate that the lady is either a *been-to* (that is she has *been to* places like London) or that she is at home with the language. To aid phonetics, a lady has to nasalise her words. Such nasalisation muffles words and makes them come out distorted and sound like those of a real Anglo-Saxon speaking (notice the structure of the white man's nose!)

A brief conversation will illustrate how a lady should conduct her speech:

A: Hi, Tessy, I've not seen you in a long time. How are *fings*? (things)

B: I'm fine. I've *jest kem beck* from *Land'n* where I spent *free* (three) months.

A: You must have had a *wond'ful* time!

B: Yea. I had a *buriful* time indeed. I feel *tweny* years younger!

A: Care *ru jein* us for *laanch*?

B: *Fanks*. I've *jest* had *somefing* to bite.

A: O.K. Nice *meering* you again.

B: Nice *meering* you too. See *ya lera*.

The beauty of how to speak is that a lady should not care whether she is actually communicating or not. It is fashionable to speak English or French to house-helps and grandmothers who

hardly understand the languages. To do this effectively, the lady must let it be seen that her local dialect or language is too difficult for her to speak, let alone understand!

The art of speaking also involves the use of one-liners, phrases and *slangs*. If someone says something and the lady is not sure of, she could ask a fast *say wot?* for a repetition. Alternatively, she could say a breezy *pard'n me*. Her father and mother shall come out as *popsy* and *momsy* respectively. When she is not sure of something, she could ask a quick *wot's det?* And when it is departure time, it is *see ya* or *ciao!*

A lady ought to know how to speak if she doesn't want to ridicule herself. When her colleague concludes a sentence with *rai*, she should be able to know that *rai* means right!

Home And Alone

A few vital tips on personal conduct when at home and alone are very necessary for the modern African lady.

Rule 1

Never answer the doorbell without first peeping through the keyhole or peer from a vantage angle on the window, to ascertain who is out there. Two types of people have a way of dropping in uninvited and becoming terrible irritants.

Group A are those female friends and acquaintances who innocently claim to have come *just to say hi* but end up treating you to a medley of unsolicited and disgusting gossip. They spoil your day and shouldn't be let in.

Group B is made up of those never-take-no-for-an-answer men who pester your life with *sweet nothings* about loving or adoring you. They too spoil the day and must not be allowed in. If a lady does, she may need some anti-riot policemen to evict them!

Rule 2

A lady need not have her bath before 4.00 pm - unless there is a *must attend* engagement on her schedule. Such engagements however, do not include going to the market or to the hairdresser's. A little bit of powder here, some lipstick there, and a most liberal sprinkling of perfume all over the body are just enough for such a trip to the market!

Rule 3

Make-up at home is not necessary. The hair should be allowed a measure of untidiness. Choice of dresses must not be fastidious; very rumpled dresses are preferable and most convenient. Better still, those that have weathered several years of constant use and must have torn at unpleasant and embarrassing places are the best. Oversized slippers of different designs should be worn.

The general appearance of a lady at home therefore must be that of a professional mourner, while her room should look as riotous as the streets of Lebanon in those days of the Syrian-Druze-Shiite-Maronite Christian battle for supremacy.

Home is the lady's castle. She is absolutely in charge. To show the extent of her unchallengeable powers, dishes can be left unwashed until they have served a mandatory 24-hour imprisonment in the washbasin. Layers of dust can be left untouched on household equipment until they get *rotten*. It's only when someone shows up unexpectedly, especially a man, that a feeble effort to clean up the house should commence, with apologies to the visitor that *I was just cleaning up when you walked in; Oh my Gad, this house is in a mess!*

Pretences have no place in a decent lady's home. It is the only place she doesn't have to *watch my weight* while eating or suddenly declaring *Oh, I'm so full* when she is in fact very hungry. Once ensconced in the home, a lady should cast aside her pride and vanity and check out some uncomplimentary remarks about her. Do her breasts actually appear like mere dots on her chest? Is it true that when she walks her behind literally crawls after her like a Nigeria Railways antiquated engine labouring to pull its coaches along? Such truths are strictly for her consumption at home. Once outside the home, the lady should feel free to claim to be the modern Monalisa!

The home is about the only place where a lady can and should *get loose*. It's her only opportunity to be herself. Outside, she spends her time living according to the standards set by the society. She must walk and talk like a lady. She cannot sit down freely for ladies are supposed to sit in a particular fashion. Even eating is a problem for everybody expects her to be a nice lady - by eating quite little, in order to keep her *wonderful shape.*

But the trouble with most ladies is that they hardly ever want to be at home alone. They would rather prefer to hear the latest tales - fashion, gossip, romance tale and novels - to having a quiet time all by themselves.

Post script: *A lady does not have to cook at home, although she must have spent a fortune to equip her kitchen. She may not know how to cook either. It really doesn't matter. There are always people to take her out!.*

What Should Make A Lady Happy

Ordinarily, a lady should always strive to wear a cheerful countenance. Only on very sombre situations should she let her face reflect her internal uneasiness or sadness. A little smile, even if forced, has a way of brightening up her face. That is why a lady must not distort or contort her face as if the whole world has crashed on her tender shoulders.

Since ladies spend a great deal of their time making themselves look attractive for men, or discussing them, it is only fair and proper for men to reciprocate by doing things that will keep ladies cheerful and happy.

There is a variety of things to do to make a lady happy. We shall go through some of them:

- A man should put himself at the lady's *disposal*. If he owns a car, for instance, he should be prepared to make it available to her upon request or even without her requesting for it. In a nutshell, the lady's wish should be a man's law.

- If a man is married and keeps a lady as his mistress, then he is under obligation to keep the lady happy at the expense of his wife and family. If this means occasionally beating up the *stupid woman* at home, he has no choice but to do just that. Miss Mistress would be thrilled to hear that Mrs Wife has been so battered by Mr Husband that she has been hospitalised!

- A lady should be allowed to get whatever she desires, despite the odds. It is left to the men to take care of those *odds*. If a lady therefore, is applying for a job for which she is not qualified, the man in charge of employment has to *wangle* it for her. All qualified men should be *disqualified*.

- If a lady is given a free hand to perform her official duties the way she wants, she shall be most happy. Nothing pleases her more than reporting late for work without a reprimand, or, having unlimited access to the boss!

- Issues or privileges and precedence also put a smile on a lady's lips. Although she might be the last person to submit her cheque at a bank, for instance, a wise male accountant should expedite action on it so that the lady is paid before others. When such privileges are accorded a lady, she feels fine.
- A lady also feels great when a man makes personal sacrifices to please her. If she wants to celebrate her birthday in grand style and her man is in financial difficulty, it is up to him to scout for money for her to accomplish her proposal. Indeed, a man's love for his lady can be measured on that score!
- When two or more men clash over who is her rightful lover, a lady also feels O.K.
- No matter what happens, a man should avoid criticising a lady. She is sad when told that what she did in her infinite wisdom is ridiculous or disjointed. A perfect gentleman must not criticise a lady. She should be allowed *to be herself!*
- A lady is also made happy when her policeman, army, navy, airforce or *big man* boyfriend deals ruthlessly with whoever displeases her!

No sane man should pray to encounter an unhappy lady. The experience is usually sad and unforgettable. That is why making ladies happy should be part of the high points on men's agenda!!

A Lady's Prayer

A modern African lady is usually too pre-occupied with the very serious and complicated business of looking pretty and attractive that she hardly has time for such extraneous things as kneeling down to pray. Nonetheless, she manages to carve out time - somehow - to remember God, especially in times of need.
This is how her prayer might go:
"Dear God,
"I know you must be uncontrollably angry that I haven't communicated with you in a long time. I apologise. I sincerely do. It's one of those things that happen in a young lady's life.

"By the way, if you don't mind my language, I've always wanted to ask you one question: why did you choose to create me with more intelligence than beauty? I suppose you know all things, including the fact that the people of this world prefer beauty to intelligence. To have sent me here with a face that is like something out of one of those Steven Spielberg's horror movies is quite unfair. Anyway, thy will be done.

"I also want to report my boss to you. This man wants to go out with me but I've told him to forget it on a number of occasions, yet he won't give up. How do I deal with him, especially now that he is subtly telling me that my job is on the line? And you know that good jobs are hard to come by these austere days. I leave everything in thine hands.

"Before I forget, there is a special favour I ask of thee. There is this special Yves St. Laurent bathroom set I would like to own. It is the vogue amongst ladies and it is humiliating not to have it. I hear the set is relatively cheaper in Brussels than London. And the price is about US$ 500. Now, how do I raise that kind of money? You certainly know how much I earn. And I don't want to debase my womanhood in order to buy it. Dear God, please help me find a solution to this problem. I'm sure you can't stand your child being the object of ridicule amongst her colleagues. I need that Yves St. Laurent set. Badly.

"I must confess that I'm a little sad. My boyfriend, Tony, has been behaving in a rather queer way these days. I can't put my finger on what is actually wrong. I do know however that there is one silly girl called Tessy who is *blowing his mind* at the moment. But I also know that this is a mere phase every man goes through. So, what is actually wrong with my Tony? Please help me solve this riddle. You know I sincerely love him and wouldn't want to lose him; certainly not to that tart who hangs around him like an insect trapped in a pool of adhesive. Besides, in these days of AIDS, Ebola virus, Rift Valley Fever and the like, you never can know what might accidentally come my way due to no fault of mine. I leave everything in your hands.

"Let me also reiterate my earlier plea to let me get a good husband. Tony would be O.K. for me, but may thy will be done. You

who knows the minds of all men should know the type of man I deserve. I don't want to end up like my friend Betty who fell into the hands of that monster who calls himself her husband.

"Thank you, Lord, that I'm not like most ladies in town who know nothing about shame. Take Angela for an example. She is no better than a prostitute. I'm happy I'm not like her.

"Dear God, save me from my enemies. Give me the grace to be graceful in all I do. Help me to get promoted above my colleagues in the office and make me the envy of all ladies.

"One last thing. There is one rich man who has shown an interest in me. I don't know whether he is boasting or not but he promised to sponsor mefor a two-week vacation in Europe next summer. May he keep to his word. I really do need a vacation. My colleagues usually brag about having visited this and that place. I want to say the same thing too when they next flaunt their travels.

"All this I ask in your only Son's name - Amen."

www.ingramcontent.com/pod-product-compliance
Lightning Source LLC
Chambersburg PA
CBHW071228160426
43196CB00012B/2449